MW01007473

No More Dating in the Dark

How to Navigate Dating Relationships
in the Light of Biblical Principles

Kenneth Harper

Copyright © 2020 by **Kenneth Harper**

Renown Publishing
www.renownpublishing.com

No More Dating in the Dark / Kenneth Harper
ISBN-13: 978-1-952602-23-8

I dedicate this book to those who are thinking about getting into a serious relationship and those who are thinking about taking the next step in their relationship. You are continually on my mind and in my heart.

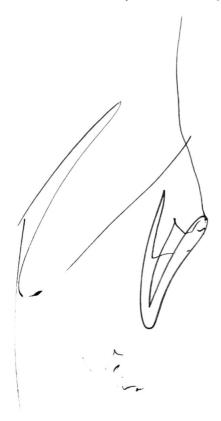

No book is the product of just its author. It is built upon the influence and outpouring of those who have gone before us and those who remain. This grateful acknowledgement must be given for those who have shaped, in some way, the contents of this book.

First, to my wife, Gail, my partner in life, love, and ministry—without your support, guidance, and willingness to follow God in our journey, I would be incomplete. I love you.

To my children—thank you for providing insight into how your generation thinks, which served as inspiration for writing this book.

Malaka—thank you for your support and encouragement. You provided innovative ideas that led to this book being launched.

To Janessa, my administrative assistant—thank you. Your hard work is much appreciated!

To my family at Channel of Grace—thank you for challenging, encouraging, and praying for me. Continue to follow God in all you do. Remember that our goal is to continue reaching and enriching lives! Blessings to each of you.

I have known Pastor Kenneth Harper for over 30 years and have seen him flourish as a youth pastor, pastor, friend, and more importantly, a great husband and father. In his book, "No More Dating in the Dark", this man of God offers practical, yet profound advice and biblical revelation on the topic of dating and relationships. Pastor Harper sheds light on a much neglected topic in the church, as he shares wisdom-filled counsel that can ensure dating and marital success for any single person desiring to please God. I highly recommend this book for all who are truly serious about relationships

Bishop William A. Lee, Jr., International Revivalist and Urban Ministry Consultant, Church of God, Cleveland, Tennessee

CONTENTS

Are You Prepared?

Are you spiritually ready, spiritually whole, and spiritually prepared to live with another person for the rest of your life? This is a question Christians need to begin to ask themselves. After over 4,000 hours of listening to people's pain in relationships during nineteen years of serving as a youth pastor and providing marital and premarital counseling, I would say that many are not prepared.

Why don't we put sixteen-year-olds in the driver's seat of a car without education and tests? Because they're completely unprepared. Yet many of us throw our children—and many of our parents threw us—into dating relationships without any kind of training and sometimes without input.

We serve a covenant-keeping God, yet we do not always view marriage as a covenant, nor do we approach dating as an effort to find a person to whom we will make a lifelong commitment. We have fun. We date for entertainment, not necessarily to build a relationship. It's important to understand the process of how to approach and evaluate a dating relationship.

Wearing the wrong shoes can cause a misfit, sore feet, and sloppy walking that rubs our feet and causes blisters. We don't put on our shoes in the dark. We turn on the light so we can make sure that they fit. However, many people risk going into a dating relationship completely unseeing, even willfully ignorant, allowing emotions and lust to guide a lifelong decision.

We have to be willing to look at a dating relationship in the light of God's Word. Otherwise, "the light you think you have is actually darkness, [and] how deep that darkness is!" (Matthew 6:23). On the other hand, Jesus said, "If you are filled with light, with no dark corners, then your whole life will be radiant, as though a floodlight were filling you with light" (Luke 11:36). That's what we want for our dating relationships. We want to see clearly what we're walking into.

Many Christian dating books don't unpack the details of the bonding process or the three-fold connection that takes place in our spirit, soul, and body, but this book does. Use it as a reference tool. Meditate on the principles shared here and allow them to work inside you.

This book provides a workbook section after each chapter that will allow you to reflect on the content and apply it to your own life and situation. Pull out your Bible, too, and fill yourself with its wisdom. Educating yourself, turning on the light of the Word as you enter a dating relationship, and learning to recognize the Holy Spirit's gentle nudging will equip you to evaluate effectively whether the other person is right for you.

Part One: Educate

CHAPTER ONE

Turn on the Light

Many Christians today walk blindly into relationships, unclear on how to build, experience, and sustain a relationship God's way. We see in the biblical story of Ruth and Boaz that Ruth acted honorably in accordance with her culture (Ruth 3:11). Naomi said that Boaz was a man of his word (Ruth 3:18). Each person acted in an upright way toward the other. As described in the wisdom writings of Proverbs, "the godliness of good people rescues them; the ambition of treacherous people traps them" (Proverbs 11:6).

Generational cycles may need to be broken concerning how we enter relationships with members of the opposite sex. It should come as no surprise that often these cycles have to do with lack of trust in God and His plan for our lives.

Current statistics reveal a crisis in marriages today. More than two million marriages take place in the United States every year, and millions more people marry every year throughout the world, but "about 40 to 50 percent of married couples in the United States divorce."[1] These facts indicate the unhealthy state of marriages today. I believe that the reason for this crisis is a lack of understanding of the dynamics of dating and relationship building. How do we make dating a productive endeavor that is pleasing to a covenant-keeping God?

First, we need to define what constitutes a dating relationship. Two people are in a dating relationship when they are in the early stages of a committed relationship and are getting to know one another. Many people date for pleasure, without thought of dating's purpose.

When I was in the military, I learned to operate in darkness, but one morning I didn't use those skills very well. I went into the kitchen to put on my tennis shoes. I had the same color and type of tennis shoes as someone else in the family. Both pairs of shoes were lying together on the floor, side by side. I put my left foot in one of the shoes, but it was too tight. He wears a smaller size than I do, and I had put on the wrong shoe. The thought occurred to me: *Turn on the light.*

Some Christians are dating like that. If you date in the dark, you are going to end up with a misfit. You're going to go out with the wrong people. It doesn't work to build a relationship in the dark. The church can help us to make the right decisions by giving us spiritual knowledge from the Bible. Without this knowledge, we will make the wrong decisions. We turn on the light to make sure that we are putting on our shoes correctly. In the same way, we need the light of the Bible to see how to approach dating relationships in a healthy way.

The Bible has a lot to say about darkness. Paul wrote, "For once you were full of darkness, but now you have light from the Lord. So live as people of light! ... Take no part in the worthless deeds of evil and darkness; instead, expose them" (Ephesians 5:8, 11). Men love darkness more than light. Don't go toward the darkness.

In another letter, Paul wrote, "The night is far spent, the day is at hand: let us therefore cast off the works of darkness, and let us put on the armour of light" (Romans 13:12 KJV). As God's children, we are to use His light to expose the darkness. Light helps us to understand darkness. You can turn on the light of His Word to guide you as you enter a dating relationship.

The apostle John said that darkness cannot comprehend or understand light. He said, "The light shines in the darkness, and the darkness can never extinguish it" (John 1:5). John further cautioned that "people loved the darkness more than the light, for their actions were evil" (John 3:19). But we are not in the darkness; we are in the light (1 Thessalonians 5:4–5). The light will penetrate the darkness. God's Word helps us to untangle the knots of relationships and feelings.

WORKBOOK

Chapter One Questions

Question: [1] What is your mindset when you enter a dating relationship? [2] Are you intentional or just seeing what will happen? [3] Is there a purpose behind your dating beyond having a good time? [4] Are there examples within your family or among your friends that you want to avoid or emulate?

[1] To really get to know the person (you) and learn them in every way. [2] All is intentional and prayed on. [3] Yes there is. To understand her but, to understand what a good time is for us. [4] For sure! At this stage of my life followings my families example are poor. Due to this I more follow "The Voice" rather then other.

Question: [1] What does it mean to date within the light instead of in darkness? [2] What type of people should you be pursuing, and what type of people should you be avoiding? [3] What qualities do you think should characterize a Christian dating relationship?

[1.] To date without fear of secrets or fear of heart break. To both date by faith, still putting the Lord first. [2.] Pursuing we'll not anyone but myself if not... (You) Avoid well anyone that comes my way that is "sick". Has problem that I don't have time for. [3.] God fearing, open to loving "in light", pushing one another to seek God for themselves, acceptance and forgiveness.

Action: Read the story of <u>Ruth</u> and <u>Boaz</u> in the short <u>Old Testament</u> book of Ruth. Make a list of the qualities each of them exhibited. How did their underlying character give strength and success to their relationship?

_____

_____

_____

_____

Chapter One Notes

_____

_____

_____

_____

_____

_____

_____

_____

_____

_____

_____

_____

_____

_____

_____

_____

_____

_____

_____

_____

_____

_____

_____

CHAPTER TWO

Relationships and Feelings

Yes, guys, this chapter is for us, too.

Fiction writers say that each character has a wound, or knot, that affects how he or she interacts with others. It is time to heal our wounds.) We might visit a doctor more than once and not be healed. (Time doesn't heal wounds. God heals wounds.) We have to involve ourselves in the process of healing our wounds. Some of us have wounds from twenty years ago, forty years ago, or even fifty years ago. If time were going to heal those wounds, they would be healed by now.

As a pastor, I counsel people in their relationships. Anna, a young wife-to-be, sat on the couch in my office in tears. Her fiancé, Christopher, wasn't sure that he wanted to go through with the marriage because he wasn't sure that he wanted to submit to the principles of God's Word regarding marriage. Anna apologized for crying. I looked at her and said, "Don't worry about it. I'm fine. This is what God trained me for, to walk with people through the emotional things we deal with. Don't worry."

A text came in at five o'clock in the morning. I checked the number and saw that it was a text from Christopher: "Can I talk to you?"

I said, "Sure," and asked how he was doing.

He said, "Can we go for lunch? No one has ever challenged me like this before in my life. No one has challenged me to remain pure. No one has challenged me to be dedicated. No one has challenged me to open up and expose how I'm really feeling in an open forum like this. I'm a man's man, and this may be too much."

I reassured him that the wisdom I wanted to share with him had the power to transform his marriage.

Christopher sat and ate lunch with me. He apologized to me and told me that he appreciated my words so much. I told him that I needed him to come back to my office with Anna, and he agreed.

Christopher met me in my office, smiling. Anna came in, also smiling.

I counseled Christopher that God had placed Anna in his life because Anna had the seeds to his destiny. As a supportive helpmate, she could empower him as an individual and the two of them as a couple in keeping the covenant and ministry God planned for them. God included emotions in the package that makes up who we are. I told Christopher that he was destined for greatness because Anna had the seeds for that greatness. She would help him to launch out. We can't minimize the effect a godly woman and her insights into emotions will have on our lives.

Through counseling, Christopher learned that

remaining pure in submission to God's way of building the relationship between him and his future wife was the best way to grow closer. This was against his belief and against everything he'd done in previous relationships, but I challenged him to try doing things God's way. I told him that if he remained pure and held God's precepts sacred, he would be rewarded with a strong bond with his soon-to-be wife. One of the things Christopher discovered through our counseling sessions was that he had never tuned in to Anna's emotions.

After Christopher and Anna came back from their honeymoon, he said, "Pastor, thank you so much for the insight and wisdom you provided. One of the things I learned was missing between Anna and me was that I was totally separated from my emotions. I really thought sex and physical activity would bring us closer together."

When we build relationships God's way, we learn how to be vulnerable with each other on an emotional level and truly connect. Men and women alike need to learn how to unpack their emotions and be willing to peel back layers and layers of emotion to get at the truth of who we are.

Emotions Help to Develop Our Relationships

Emotions are important in a relationship. They are part of turning on the light to let the other person see who we truly are. We do this when we tell the other person how we feel. Sharing our emotions enables us to make sure that a dating relationship is a good long-term fit.

A woman appreciates it when a man tells her how he feels. The worst thing we can do in a relationship is not share our emotions. I'm not saying that we should cry every day, but if there is something hurting deep within, the other person needs to know that. Each person needs to feel part of the other's life. One way to do this is to pray together often.

Prayer Strengthens a Dating Relationship

We share our lives when we pray together. Sometimes when we pray together, we reveal to our respective partner things we didn't realize were bothering us. Prayer brings God into the relationship and strengthens it. The Bible says, "A person standing alone can be attacked and defeated, but two can stand back-to-back and conquer. Three are even better, for a triple-braided cord is not easily broken" (Ecclesiastes 4:12). External circumstances will attack a relationship, and storms will come against it, but two people joined in prayer to God will draw on His peace and strength in any situation.

Stress Impacts Our Relationships

Prayer can bring healing, but keeping our emotions inside impacts our relationships in a different way. Sometimes when difficult or stressful things happen in our lives, we choose to hide how we really feel about the situation. Things that may strain a relationship include health, family, financial, or personality issues.

A Word to Men

Men, we need to learn healthy ways of dealing with our emotions. There is nothing wrong with saying, "I hurt" or "I feel frustrated." We have to unpack these feelings. If we don't, our kids may also grow up hiding or ignoring their feelings. Guess how they're going to treat their wives or husbands? They will likely be detached and seemingly uninterested. This unhealthy pattern of being unemotional may be reinforced, as it can continue from one generation to the next.

A Word to Women

It's hard for men to share their feelings. I believe that it goes against our nature. Our society places value on men being independent and strong, without an emphasis on emotions. Rather than intentionally hiding their emotions from their wives, men often don't share because they haven't learned how to verbalize what they feel inside.

In our home, we share our emotions. I have cried in front of my son. I have said to him, "I messed up. I did some things that were wrong." I've prayed before my children, "God, forgive me." I want my kids to see the role of feelings in relationships. I want to model for them how to talk about emotions.

If you are not in a relationship, someone else can't tell you what to do. Moreover, you are under no obligation to share your emotions. However, once you are in a relationship with someone else, you have to be willing to be submissive and yield, first to God and then to your partner.

Paul said it this way: "For ye were sometimes darkness, but now are ye light in the Lord: walk as children of light" (Ephesians 5:8 KJV) and "[submit] yourselves one to another in the fear of God" (Ephesians 5:21 KJV). We have to yield our will to one another, and this includes our willingness to share our feelings. Emotions are powerful, and they play an important role in how we connect with other people, which we'll take a closer look at in the next chapter.

WORKBOOK

Chapter Two Questions

Question: What unhealed wounds do you carry? If you are in a relationship, what wounds does your partner have? What are some practical ways you can find healing for these things from the Lord rather than looking to each other to fix your brokenness?

1. "I still feel deeply about not waking up sooner as a man & husband. Along with pain from my father not teaching me how to be a man. 2. She hold a life-time of wounds that only God can heal. 3. We can start by praying from the heart, and seeking help. Not stopping till we have a hold on ourselves. "Seek first the Kingdom of God."

Question: How open are you in sharing your emotions with your partner? If you are not currently in a relationship, do you share your emotions with a close friend or family member? If this is difficult for you, what is one small step you can take toward beginning a habit of sharing your feelings? Are you a "safe place" for others, especially your partner, to share their emotions without fear of judgment or derision?

I'm not sure due to me being changed by this stage of life, but she know how I feel. 2nd. Yes. 3. Learning the right time to speak & when to shut up. 4. Yes she is my heart and only God, can judge and knows my heart.

Action: If you are in a dating relationship, begin praying with your partner. The frequency and depth of your prayer times should coordinate with the depth of your relationship. Praying together before meals is appropriate for a new or casual relationship while a focused and scheduled prayer time should be in place for an engaged or married couple.

_____

_____

_____

_____

_____

_____

_____

_____

_____

_____

Chapter Two Notes

CHAPTER THREE

Connections in Relationships

We are three-part beings: spirit, soul, and body. When we connect with God and other people, we do so on all three levels. We cannot truly connect with others until we enter into a relationship with God. Jesus said that "the first and greatest commandment" is to grow closer to God by loving Him "with all your heart, all your soul, and all your mind" (Matthew 22:37–38). Developing your relationship with God will then help you to develop a deeper dating relationship.

Relationship with God

Religion and a relationship with God are two different things. Jesus Christ came so that we could have a relationship with Him. What, then, is religion? Religion is important because it deals with our belief system. Beliefs produce behavior: right actions or wrong actions.

What do we believe about God? To know God and

have a relationship with Him, we must have an understanding of who He is. Our relationship with Him comes as a result of what Jesus Christ accomplished on the cross. When He died, He paid the penalty for our sins and opened the way for us to come back into a right relationship with God. Once you accept His work on the cross and ask for His forgiveness, you come into relationship with Him. This relationship produces abundant life (John 10:10). Salvation is powerful. It has movement. It has life in it.

In his letter to the church at Thessalonica, Paul talked about the time when Jesus will come for those who are in relationship with Him. He said something powerful: "Now may the God of peace make you holy in every way, and may your whole spirit and soul and body be kept blameless until our Lord Jesus Christ comes again" (1 Thessalonians 5:23). In every way? Yes, in every way. Each person has a spirit and a soul that live in a body.

There is a connection in every relationship. Even in the infancy stage, as we begin to grow, there is a connection. In every relationship, there has to be a spiritual connection because we are spiritual beings. The reason we are spiritual is not only because we are created in the image of God (Genesis 1:27), but also because we are in Christ and connected to Christ. As a result of that, we are creatures who have His Spirit living in us.

Spiritual Connection in a Relationship

As Christians, we have a spiritual connection to God. What does this spiritual aspect of our being look like in a dating relationship? You need to invite God into your relationship. The Old Testament book of Ecclesiastes observes that "two are better than one; because they have a good reward for their labour" (Ecclesiastes 4:9 KJV). Together, two can be more successful than one person alone, but three are even stronger. A cord of three "is not easily broken" (Ecclesiastes 4:12).

God has to be at the center of every relationship. We have to invite God in and let Him be the Lord of our relationship. When He is the strength of the relationship, we can function at a certain capacity and be a blessing to our partner.

Physical Connection in a Relationship

We don't practice sex while dating because once we are in a relationship with God, we want to please Him and live favorably with Him. We invite God into our relationship. Our holy God calls us to live pure and holy lives before Him.

Paul explained how this looks: "When you follow the desires of your sinful nature, the results are very clear: sexual immorality, impurity, lustful pleasures, … envy, drunkenness, wild parties, and other sins like these. Let me tell you again, as I have before, that anyone living that sort of life will not inherit the Kingdom of God" (Galatians 5:19, 21). Paul also wrote, "Let there be no sexual immorality, impurity, or greed among you. Such sins have no place among God's people" (Ephesians 5:3).

In the previous chapter, we noted that prayer strengthens a dating relationship. Perhaps the most important way to apply this principle is in the area of physical connection. As God told the Israelites, "if my people who are called by my name will humble themselves and pray and seek my face and turn from their wicked ways, I will hear from heaven and will forgive their sins and restore their land" (2 Chronicles 7:14).

There is humility in praying. Sometimes there is a complication, and we need God to handle it. We need wisdom from heaven to deal with the physical aspect of our relationship. When we humble ourselves to pray, we can say, "God, I can't do this without You. I need You to help me." He wants us to seek His face and turn from our wicked ways. There are most likely changes we will have to make.

It's important for us to understand this truth and to teach it to others, including the next generation. My goal is to shine the light on these things to keep Christians from dating in the dark. Every person has a place, and that's his or her land, or environment. We need God to heal that land. To receive His healing, we must humble ourselves, pray, and seek His face.

Our environment and upbringing impact how we view and approach physical connection in a relationship. We all come into a relationship with a value system. We learn these things from the culture in which we were raised. When we invite God into our relationship, we need to pray for God's will. We put aside our upbringing and human value system and submit to God's will. This is why we ask for God's help when we pray. Our spiritual connection to God and relationship with Him will guide us as we recreate our value system from what we learned growing up to what God wants.

Soulful Connection in a Relationship

It's important to have a soulful connection in your dating relationship. In his letter to Gaius, a church leader, John wrote, "Beloved, I wish above all things that thou mayest prosper and be in health, even as thy soul prospereth" (3 John 1:2 KJV). *Soul* here refers to what makes each of us an individual person, such as our desires, emotions, affections, and passions.[2] To prosper, our soul requires meaningful connections.

The soul is made up of three parts: the mind, the will, and the emotions. Our mind is the first aspect of our soul. We have to connect with another person at the intellectual level. This has nothing to do with our mental ability, skills, or educational degree, but rather our thoughts in general. We make a conscious decision to connect with another person, being "likeminded, ... being of one accord," and considering the other person above ourselves (Philippians 2:2–3 KJV). We choose to connect with the other person by thinking of him or her and placing that person's needs before our own.

Our will is an important part of our soul. This is closely tied to the mind. We make a decision to act on our faith in God. James taught that our desires can lead us astray into sin (James 1:13–15). Our desires often determine how we behave, and this usually affects our interactions with other people.

The soul also consists of our emotions. Some people think that men don't have emotions, but the truth is that we have never learned how to handle our feelings in a biblical way. We have been raised not to cry. That isn't healthy for a man. In fact, it leads to the reality that men commit suicide more often than women.[3] Tears of sorrow can open us to God's healing and work in our lives.

The book of Proverbs tells us that a man can trust his woman with his heart and his secrets (Proverbs 31:11). Sometimes a man wants to talk, but other times he can't handle his emotions. If he can't handle whatever he's going through, he isn't going to share it with his woman.

Why is handling emotions so important? The highway to the soul of a woman is her emotions. It is not sex. Though the impression that women speak thousands more words a day than men has been disproven empirically,[4] it surely can seem that way in some relationships! There's nothing wrong with this, however; it's how God has made each of us. Women, maybe more than men, need a place to unpack their feelings.

At some point, you will meet someone with whom you believe you can share these types of connections: spiritual, physical, and soulful, or emotional. You will desire to enter into a dating relationship with that person. But what exactly is a dating relationship?

WORKBOOK

Chapter Three Questions

Question: Describe your relationship with God. How are you connected to Him, through both the gift of salvation and an ongoing walk in His Spirit? Is God the Lord of your dating relationship? How can you tell?

As far as connection, words can't discribe how close we are. Due to this salvation I know healing is real. Lord Papa is King of this dating and I know bcuz it could be worst. N I'm thankful. My eye are open

Question: [1]How can a dating couple intentionally and purposefully move from a relationship based on mutual activities or gatherings to a true soul connection? [2]What are some ways to encourage this without forcing it?

[1] *I think it'd be a connection that turns from words to deep actions.*

[2] *Taking your time*
Loving slow but hard
Just having fun and being content with your blessings

Action: How should Christians determine what is an acceptable physical relationship before marriage? Should displays of affection, such as holding hands or kissing, be prohibited? Should anything short of intercourse be acceptable, such as "sexting" or spending the night? Write out your standards for sexuality based on biblical principles and the wise counsel of godly mentors. (This topic will be discussed in greater depth in chapter 8.)

This is something I'd love to talk about.

All is okay if your marriage
is still at hand.

Chapter Three Notes

We cant be anything
if we don't have a
true relationship with
the Lord.

I'm rightous because
Jesus died for us. So we
cant become rightous, because
we are by his grace.

CHAPTER FOUR

Maturity in Relationships

We enter into a dating relationship when we spend time with another person for the purpose of getting to know him or her better. In this chapter, we'll see how immaturity affects relationships and consider God's purpose for dating: to prepare two people for marriage.

Any time there is immaturity in a relationship, there will be dismay. Two people in such a relationship don't know how to do life together due to immaturity. The apostle Paul said, "When I was a child, I spoke and thought and reasoned as a child. But when I grew up, I put away childish things" (1 Corinthians 13:11). Marriage is for mature people capable of Christlike love, so we have to grow up.

We mature in three areas. The first is to become mature in our thinking. Paul wrote:

And be not conformed to this world: but be ye transformed by the renewing of your mind, that ye may prove what is that good, and acceptable, and perfect, will of God.

For I say, through the grace given unto me, to every man
that is among you, not to think of himself more highly than
he ought to think; but to think soberly, according as God
hath dealt to every man the measure of faith.
—Romans 12:2–3 *(KJV)*

This leads to maturity in our reasoning. We see our need for God and His salvation. God said through Isaiah to those who strayed from Him: "Come now, and let us reason together ... Though your sins be as scarlet, they shall be as white as snow; though they be red like crimson, they shall be as wool" (Isaiah 1:18 KJV).

Finally, we must grow up in our speaking. James, the half-brother of Jesus, had quite a bit to say about taming the tongue. He summarized it this way: "Indeed, we all make many mistakes. For if we could control our tongues, we would be perfect and could also control ourselves in every other way" (James 3:2).

Maturity in relationships has everything to do with the Bible's teaching about these three areas: thought, reasoning, and speech. When we allow God to shine the light of His truth in our lives, we see ourselves as we really are, people loved by God and in need of His salvation. Once we receive His salvation, His love pours through us to help us grow in all ways, including our speech. We'll strive to follow Paul's advice: "Don't use foul or abusive language. Let everything you say be good and helpful, so that your words will be an encouragement to those who hear them" (Ephesians 4:29).

It isn't difficult to imagine that it would take a person years to recover from a situation or relationship affected by immaturity in one or more of these areas. These experiences may impact our destination or the steps we take toward the purpose God has for our lives.

Immaturity in Dating Relationships

A young lady in a relationship may have a mothering instinct. Some guys didn't have good mothers. They weren't properly mothered by their mothers, and now they need that mother's love. These guys often become sexually active very early. They are looking for a love they never had before. They want a woman to take care of them. That is a red flag. Don't go down that street.

The caution is for women as well. A woman who didn't feel love in her family may be drawn to this type of man because she wants the emotional closeness she finds in sex. She also wants an outlet for the natural nurturing love instilled in her by God. Caring for a man draws on that.

How can a woman be taken care of by a man who won't go to work and just wants to stay home and play video games while she takes care of him? Such a relationship consists of two broken people, and they often don't grow beyond this level of emotional maturity. Instead of helping each other to become better people, they each support the other's dysfunction, which may, in turn, affect other people and break them.

Paul admonished men to "love your wives, just as Christ loved the church. He gave up his life for her" (Ephesians 5:25). A dating relationship is preparation for marriage. How people treat each other in a dating relationship is a good indication of how they will treat each other in marriage.

Someone in a dating relationship may be looking for the other person to take care of him or her. When a baby is born, the woman falls in love with that baby immediately. God created women to be nurturing to take care of their children. There's nothing wrong with being or having a loving mother; that's God's will for us. But it's not good to be in a relationship with someone who is still tied to a parent in an unhealthy way.

Some people grew up differently. A man might have learned to curse a woman or treat her with disrespect. Some women want someone a little rough around the edges. Some people are constantly apologizing, as if everything they do is wrong. Who taught them this? We learn these things in the environment in which we were raised.

What if you find yourself in this situation? You can ask yourself whom or what you look to for love and nurturing. God is our primary source of true, unconditional love. Once we become adults and leave our parents' home, we are designed to seek and give love to and nurture another person within the context of the marriage relationship. If you see that you are not yet able to treat a dating partner in a godly way, you can seek healing through counseling. You can set a goal of personal growth and learning to be truly ready for this type of relationship.

Joseph's Dating Experience

Joseph and Mary give us a glimpse of a betrothed (dating) couple in the Bible. They were ready and willing not only to be in a relationship, but also to hear God's Word about that relationship.

Mary was engaged to Joseph. They were in a serious relationship, and she was ready to get married. Scripture tells us that "before the marriage took place, while she was still a virgin, she became pregnant through the power of the Holy Spirit" (Matthew 1:18). Mary submitted to God's will for her life, even though it would affect her relationship with Joseph (Luke 1:38).

What happened when Joseph realized that his fiancée was pregnant? Matthew wrote, "Joseph, to whom she was engaged, was a righteous man and did not want to disgrace her publicly, so he decided to break the engagement quietly" (Matthew 1:19).

This says something about Joseph's relationship with God. Joseph discovered that the girl he was engaged to was pregnant, but he understood grace and mercy. Joseph was right in his relationship with God and others, including Mary. When we accept God's forgiveness, God considers us righteous, too, through Christ's death on the cross.

Because of Joseph's relationship with God, an angel came to him in a dream. Then Joseph "did as the angel of the Lord commanded and took Mary as his wife" (Matthew 1:24). Joseph cared about Mary's reputation and honor, and he followed God's leading to marry her.

Dating as Preparation for Marriage

Part of learning maturity in a dating relationship is understanding its purpose. Dating serves as an intermediate stage between getting to know someone and entering into the covenant of marriage. It's a time to shine the light of

God's Word on the relationship to make sure that the two people in the relationship are a good fit for each other. Earlier we saw that many marriages today end in divorce. One of the main reasons for this is that couples don't always seek God's approval for their relationship. People enter into a dating relationship without fully understanding the purpose of this in-between stage and what to do in it. They may be misfits and not even know it.

In his second letter to Pastor Timothy, Paul reminded him to shine the light of God's Word on all aspects of his life: "All Scripture is inspired by God and is useful to teach us what is true and to make us realize what is wrong in our lives. It corrects us when we are wrong and teaches us to do what is right" (2 Timothy 3:16). We can read God's Word to discover characteristics of godly people and how those apply to our dating and marriage relationships. If the light of God's Word reveals that we are in a relationship that is a misfit, the Bible can also show us the right way to break up.

It's really hard to depart from relationships, for men and women both. Let's look back at the example of Joseph and Mary. Mary was in a committed relationship, planning to be married to Joseph, when she became pregnant by the Holy Spirit. Joseph was a good man, and he didn't want to subject Mary to public disgrace. He decided to break off their engagement quietly. According to the Law, Mary should have been stoned to death for the sin of adultery. Joseph loved Mary, and he wanted to break up with her privately, without harming her.

If people agree to part ways, there is a right way and a wrong way to depart the relationship. Joseph was a righteous man. People who are mature care about doing relationships right. We need to be right with the person with whom we are in a relationship. If you have determined that the relationship is a misfit and you decide to break up with the other person, there's a right way to do it.

Paul's teaching about how to live as children of light is a good starting point: "…be kind to each other, tenderhearted, forgiving one another, just as God through Christ has forgiven you" (Ephesians 4:32). In practical terms, this means that you shouldn't abruptly stop talking to the other person. This would show that you have allowed your feelings to get in the way. Take time to discuss the situation and let the other person know why you are breaking up. If it seems best, have the conversation in a public, neutral place. This will help to keep explosive feelings at bay. Have a time of prayer. Talk on the phone or text during the first week of a break-up. This is the time for the person departing the relationship to say, "I'm sorry."

If you date the wrong person, you will experience a bad fit, like wearing shoes that are either too small or too big. You will become uncomfortable in your life and in your faith. The concepts and information in the next few chapters of this book will better equip you to make healthy choices in your dating relationships.

WORKBOOK

Chapter Four Questions

Question: What are some areas where you personally need to mature? Are there ways in which your thinking, reasoning, or speaking are childish? How can growing in Christ help you to become more mature in these areas?

_____

_____

_____

_____

_____

_____

_____

_____

_____

_____

Question: What relationships were lacking or weak in your family of origin? Have you looked to a dating relationship to meet your lack? Or have you copied these unhealthy patterns because they feel more comfortable to you than stepping out in faith to do things God's way? How can you learn from the successes and/or mistakes of your family of origin while not carrying baggage from your past into your own future family?

_____

_____

_____

_____

_____

_____

_____

_____

_____

_____

_____

_____

Action: Evaluate if you have a tendency toward dating immature, emotionally needy people. Are you in such a relationship now? How can you end a "wrong fit" relationship in a godly way? Using the principles in this chapter, as well as discussion with a godly mentor, write a break-up guide for how a Christian can depart a relationship in a way that honors God and is respectful and kind to the other person.

_____

_____

_____

_____

_____

_____

_____

_____

_____

_____

Chapter Four Notes

_____

_____

_____

_____

_____

_____

_____

_____

_____

_____

_____

_____

_____

_____

_____

_____

_____

_____

_____

_____

_____

_____

Part Two: Equip

CHAPTER FIVE

First Steps

We've defined dating as two people getting to know one another in the early stages of a relationship. We've also looked at God's reason for dating: preparation for marriage. This section will shed light on how we can equip ourselves to enter a dating relationship. We turn on a light to make sure that our shoes fit properly. We also check to make sure that they are the right shoes.

We learn about different types of shoes for ease and comfort in walking. We learn which types are suitable for different purposes. Then we equip ourselves by wearing the right kind of shoe for our purpose. Throughout this book, we have used Scripture to equip us, as Paul counseled Timothy: "God uses it [Scripture] to prepare and equip his people to do every good work" (2 Timothy 3:17). Let's look at first steps that will equip you to shine the light on your dating relationships.

Tests Before Entering a Dating Relationship

In the illustration I used before, when I tried to put on my shoes in the kitchen and reached for the wrong ones, I tested the shoes almost without thinking about it. I could immediately tell that something wasn't right. If I had turned on the light, I could more easily have checked for a misfit.

There are two tests you should perform before entering a dating relationship. The first concerns a person's background. It's important to do the homework. You would do the same thing before entering a business relationship. You want to know what you're getting yourself into. Part of doing the homework is finding out whether or not the other person is already married. Even if you have determined not to play games in dating, you don't want to date the wrong person unintentionally.

It's a good idea to check out how the other person lives. What this includes will depend somewhat on what you prefer in a potential partner. You may want to know more about the other person's educational, social, or economic background. Perhaps you wish to know more about how that person lives on a personal level.

You can learn about someone's character and background by talking to his or her friends and family members. If you're considering dating someone you have met casually, this may be a little more difficult, but it's a good way to learn more about that person. When you talk to friends or family members, you may also learn about a person's personal habits. Another way to learn how a person lives is to spend time together in casual, informal group settings.

The second test is even more important. No matter where you met the person you're considering dating, whether at church or elsewhere, you need to test his or her spirit. What priority does that person place on the Lord? Check to see that he or she approaches life the way Paul advised: "...whether you eat or drink, or whatever you do, do it all for the glory of God" (1 Corinthians 10:31).

The other aspect of testing someone's spirit is observing how he or she treats others. We all have a selfish nature, but Paul encouraged believers, "Don't be selfish; don't try to impress others. Be humble, thinking of others as better than yourselves. Don't look out only for your own interests, but take an interest in others, too" (Philippians 2:3–4). Is the other person willing to do something for you or someone else?

These tests serve an important purpose because you do not want to end up with the wrong person for life. You need to enter a new relationship with your eyes wide open and the light turned on.

Action Steps for Dating

It's important to investigate the other person before you enter a dating relationship. You want to learn about that person's character, habits, and spiritual state. As you perform these tests on people you meet, you are hoping to find a certain type of person to date. The key question, however, is: Are *you* being this type of person for *others*? This requires action on your part. You must be willing to make changes in your life, too. It's important to examine your own life to make sure that you have the same spirit—living under the Lord's leadership—that you are looking for in someone else.

You don't want your "better half." You don't want to marry a half person. You want to be someone who is a better whole in a relationship. This happens when two people are both willing to give 100% to the relationship. We cannot give only 50% and expect it to work. We must be willing to commit fully to the other person and the relationship.

How can you find the type of person God desires for you in a covenant relationship? The Bible says (in our twenty-first-century understanding) to look for a man or a woman who has a soul and a heart that belong totally to the Lord, someone who is under the Lord's leadership. The story of Abraham, his trusted servant, Rebekah, and Isaac, recorded in Genesis 24, is an example of this principle.

Abraham sent his servant to find a wife for his son, Isaac (Genesis 24:4). Before the servant left, he clarified the terms with Abraham, and Abraham set the stage for this journey of faith. Abraham told his servant, "For the LORD, the God of heaven, who took me from my father's house and my native land, solemnly promised to give this land to my descendants. He will send his angel ahead of you, and he will see to it that you find a wife there for my son" (Genesis 24:7). Your first step is to believe that God will go before you as you seek a suitable person to date in a relationship that honors God's purposes.

The servant "made the camels kneel beside a well just outside the town. It was evening, and the women were coming out to draw water" (Genesis 24:11). He went to a place where he could meet God-fearing women. You, too, need to look for a potential partner among the people who share your faith. You will find them in places where they gather together.

Once he was positioned by the well, Abraham's servant prayed to God.

> *"O Lord, God of my master, Abraham," he prayed. "Please give me success today, and show unfailing love to my master, Abraham. See, I am standing here beside this spring, and the young women of the town are coming out to draw water. This is my request. I will ask one of them, 'Please give me a drink from your jug.' If she says, 'Yes, have a drink, and I will water your camels, too!'—let her be the one you have selected as Isaac's wife. This is how I will know that you have shown unfailing love to my master."*
> —**Genesis 24:12–14**

He asked God for a clear indication of the one God had in mind for Isaac. It would be wise to follow his example and pray to God for success when you are dating. Pray today, not tomorrow, for success today.

One of the tests you can use to determine the suitability of a potential partner is to observe how that person treats others. Abraham's servant watched Rebekah closely to learn if she was God's answer to his prayer (Genesis 24:21). He saw that she watered the camels as promised. He watched as she returned to her family to prepare the way for his visit.

Her family wanted a little time to get used to the idea, but Abraham's servant said, "Don't delay me. The Lord has made my mission successful; now send me back so I can return to my master" (Genesis 24:55–56). They asked Rebekah, "Are you willing to go with this man?" (Genesis 24:58). She had faith to follow God's leading. This part of the story ends happily ever after: "Isaac brought Rebekah into his mother Sarah's tent, and she became his wife. He loved her deeply" (Genesis 24:67).

The heart of your potential partner, your future wife or husband, must be connected to the Lord. We stay connected to God when we seek Him and His will first in our lives. Jesus said, "I am the vine; you are the branches. Those who remain in me, and I in them, will produce much fruit. For apart from me you can do nothing" (John 15:5). Only in Him can you learn to seek and *be* the type of person God calls into a dating relationship that pleases Him. In order to ensure that your dating relationship lines up with God's purposes, we'll next consider some pitfalls to avoid when dating.

WORKBOOK

Chapter Five Questions

Question: What are some ways you can learn about a potential dating partner? What challenges are unique to getting to know a person you met at work, at church, through mutual friends, or online? How can you balance having high standards for your future partner with extending grace and not demanding perfection?

_____

_____

_____

_____

_____

_____

_____

_____

_____

Question: What are some warning signs that the other person is not truly committed to you or to the relationship? How can you watch for these signs without being constantly paranoid about the state of the relationship?

_____

_____

_____

_____

_____

_____

_____

_____

_____

_____

Action: Read the story of Isaac and Rebekah in Genesis 24. What lessons can you learn from their "dating" process and from the actions and responses of Abraham, Isaac, the servant, Rebekah, and her family? What principles from this account should still inform and influence twenty-first-century Christian dating?

_____

_____

_____

_____

_____

_____

_____

_____

_____

_____

_____

Chapter Five Notes

CHAPTER SIX

Pitfalls to Avoid

One way to shine the light on a dating relationship is to examine potential pitfalls in your approach to dating. In this way, you can check your understanding and practice of the purpose for dating.

Dating Misconceptions

It is easy to fall into misconceptions about dating. A misconception is an opinion based on our own thinking. It is an incorrect perception or way of viewing a situation. In this case, a misconception is an incorrect way of looking at dating based on faulty thinking.

A primary misconception concerning dating is that dating someone guarantees marriage to that person. That is not true. Even if you date someone, you may not get married to that person. Dating requires us to seek out different people so we can figure out who the right one is for us. God may confirm that a person you are dating is not right for you and call you not to marry that person.

Another misconception is that we should keep dating and going into relationships over and over again so we can figure out who the right one is for us. A danger of dating many people is that we can become desensitized to the hurt break-ups cause. Multiple dating relationships can also lead to lack of confidence in future relationships.

If you are praying for God to send you a husband or a wife, then you need not fall into the trap of dating a huge number of people. Dating many different people may not be the solution God has for you. You don't need to date every single person of the opposite sex you meet. God would have you bring potential dating partners before Him in prayer.

God wants us to wait on Him in hope and expectation. With the psalmist, we can say, "I am counting on the LORD; yes, I am counting on him. I have put my hope in his word" (Psalm 130:5). You can wait with an expectation to see whom God will bring into your life. You don't have to change where God has placed you in order to meet a person. He can arrange circumstances to bring about His will in your life.

Misconceptions can derail your dating from its purpose. You enter a dating relationship to get to know another person, including his or her heart motives. Dating many people doesn't really address that purpose of dating. When you start to date, you need to remember that both people are on their best behavior up front. That doesn't reveal a person's true motives. You should go into dating with your eyes open, and that means turning on the light to expose the games people play in the dark.

Games People Play

People play a lot of games when it comes to dating relationships. Some people know that they will never become fully committed to the relationship, but they give a lot of compliments, leading the other person on. All they want to do is play around. One or both people flirt with the other. People may play these games to feel better about themselves. This attitude is unfair to the other person, who may expect a commitment. It is a form of deceit, which should not be part of the Christian's life. Peter urged Christians in the early church to "get rid of all evil behavior. Be done with all deceit, hypocrisy, jealousy, and all unkind speech" (1 Peter 2:1). Paul said it bluntly: "...stop telling lies. Let us tell our neighbors the truth, for we are all parts of the same body" (Ephesians 4:25).

Not only do we deceive others, we deceive ourselves as well, suppressing the truth about God and who we are. We are designed to be in a covenant relationship with a person of the opposite sex. When people choose to follow their sinful nature, "God abandon[s] them to their shameful desires" (Romans 1:26). Some people date people of the same sex, which goes against the nature of how we were created. After God created everything else in all creation, "male and female he created them" (Genesis 1:27). In marriage, "a man leaves his father and mother and is joined to his wife, and the two are united into one" (Genesis 2:24).

Some people like to date married people. This game is unfair to both parties, since such a dating relationship has no purpose and can never go anywhere. The Bible speaks to this game as well, admonishing us to cut it off before such a situation ever gets started. Moses recorded God's commandments for holy living, and over half of those commands concern how we treat other people. God said, "You must not covet your neighbor's wife" (Exodus 20:17). Don't even wish that you could date someone else's spouse.

Even with all these games and potential problems in a dating relationship, some people still refuse to receive counsel. They play the game of deceiving themselves regarding the need for outside help. These people choose to deny problems in the relationship. They may not recognize signs of immaturity (as described in chapter 4) or admit when there are red flags (which will be explained in more detail in chapters 10 and 11).

It's hard to change unhealthy patterns of behavior. How can Christians stop playing games in their dating relationships? Perhaps they need to recognize if they are not truly ready or willing to pursue the purpose of a dating relationship, which is to get to know another person better to determine if they are a good fit for each other for the long-term covenant relationship of marriage.

If you don't want to commit to a dating relationship at this time or if you determine that you are in a relationship that is a bad fit, you can look back at chapter 4, where we discussed how to depart from a relationship in a godly way. If you choose to take steps toward commitment to another person in a dating relationship, we can review what God says in His Word about how to interact with other people.

Perhaps you observe someone close to you playing

games in a dating relationship. The first step is to talk prayerfully with the person about his or her relationship with God. This will indicate if there is a willingness to quit playing games. In this matter of dealing with sin, the apostle John said, "If we walk in the light, as he is in the light, we have fellowship one with another, and the blood of Jesus Christ his Son cleanseth us from all sin. If we say that we have no sin, we deceive ourselves, and the truth is not in us" (1 John 1:7–8 KJV).

Confessing sin and receiving forgiveness are heart actions. How can you help your friend or family member take the next step in changing his or her behavior? Paul gave excellent advice when he said, "If another believer is overcome by some sin, you who are godly should gently and humbly help that person back onto the right path. And be careful not to fall into the same temptation yourself" (Galatians 6:1). You can read God's Word together to shed light on how and why people play games in dating relationships. One way to help one another become more like Jesus is to be willing to mentor and be mentored.

WORKBOOK

Chapter Six Questions

Question: What wrong thinking leads some people to become "serial daters"? What are some specific ways you can seek God's will about a relationship before committing to it?

_____

_____

_____

_____

_____

_____

_____

_____

_____

_____

Question: Describe a time when you dated someone who was playing games. How did it make you feel when you realized the truth about your partner? How can you apply the golden rule (Matthew 7:12) to your dating life?

_____

_____

_____

_____

_____

_____

_____

_____

_____

_____

_____

Action: Ask a friend who knows you well to call you out if he or she observes you playing games in a dating relationship. Repent and ask forgiveness from God and your partner. Seek wisdom from God's Word about how to build a relationship on truth and in the light.

_____

_____

_____

_____

Chapter Six Notes

_____

_____

_____

_____

_____

_____

_____

_____

_____

_____

_____

_____

_____

_____

_____

_____

_____

_____

_____

_____

_____

_____

CHAPTER SEVEN

Mentoring

What does it mean to mentor someone or to be mentored? A mentor provides wise, loyal advice and serves as a teacher or a coach. The Bible says that "we are surrounded by ... a huge crowd of witnesses to the life of faith" (Hebrews 12:1). We can benefit from the experience previous generations may have handed down to us. Perhaps they didn't say anything aloud, but we have observed what worked and didn't work in the dating relationships of others. We may also choose to ask experienced, wise people for their advice and counsel concerning dating.

On the other hand, maybe God has asked us to mentor someone who is about to enter or is already in a dating relationship. We may feel called to be "witnesses" who tell what we have heard and seen. We can share our experiences and what we have learned from observing dating relationships.

Often, but not always, a mentor is someone who is

older than the person who is being mentored. These people have had more time to learn life's lessons. Paul wrote, "Teach the older women to live in a way that honors God. … These older women must train the younger women to love their husbands and their children, to live wisely and be pure, to work in their homes, to do good, and to be submissive to their husbands. Then they will not bring shame on the word of God" (Titus 2:3–5). This applies to men mentoring other men as well. In the same passage, Paul wrote, "Similarly, encourage the young men to be self-controlled. In everything set them an example by doing what is good. In your teaching show integrity" (Titus 2:6–7 NIV). Those who are in a position to pass along what they have learned about dating relationships should do so with integrity and transparency before God.

A seasoned voice in your ear is good to have. It is unwise to choose someone who is always going to agree with you to be your mentor. You want someone who has a little seasoning and has been walking with God for a little bit, someone who knows the Spirit, who knows the mind of the Spirit. That person desires to live in a way that pleases God. In this way, we can fulfill Jesus' words: "You are the light of the world—like a city on a hilltop that cannot be hidden" (Matthew 5:14).

When we agree to mentor, or come alongside, two people to counsel them regarding dating, our goal should be to lead them gently to God's principles for living. This requires us to be familiar with God's Word. According to Paul, we should "carefully determine what pleases the Lord" and "be careful how [we] live" (Ephesians 5:10, 15). He wrote, "Don't live like fools, but like those who are wise. … Don't act thoughtlessly, but understand what the Lord wants you to do. … [And] be filled with the Holy Spirit…" (Ephesians 5:15, 17–18).

Paul also cautioned us not to make "provision for the flesh" (Romans 13:14 KJV). We are not to think about ways to indulge our sinful nature. As believers, we are filled with the Spirit. Although we may have a goal of practicing good behaviors, we still have that sin nature. We need to make an effort to stop feeding that nature. Whatever we feed most in our lives will determine how we behave. Therefore, it's important to set boundaries in dating relationships and surrender those boundaries to God.

WORKBOOK

Chapter Seven Questions

Question: If you are married, what wisdom do you have to pass on to those who are still in the dating and waiting season? If you are single, in what areas would it be helpful to have a mentor to guide you as you navigate dating relationships and seek the right person to marry?

_____

_____

_____

_____

_____

_____

_____

_____

_____

Question: Why do you think it is hard for many single people to find and ask someone to be a mentor? What hinders married people from stepping into that role? How can the church and mature believers help to make these connections, and what would a successful mentorship look like?

_____

_____

_____

_____

_____

_____

_____

_____

_____

_____

_____

_____

Action: Read Proverbs 5. What do you see in this chapter (and throughout Proverbs) about being teachable, particularly in the area of relationships? Ask a few people close to you how you are doing with being teachable, listening to wise counsel, and receiving truth into your life.

_____

_____

Chapter Seven Notes

_____

_____

_____

_____

_____

_____

_____

_____

_____

_____

_____

_____

_____

_____

_____

_____

_____

_____

_____

_____

_____

_____

_____

_____

CHAPTER EIGHT

Boundaries in Relationships

We've talked about how turning on a light helps us to avoid a misfit in a dating relationship. We also turn on a light to see where we're going. Without a light, it's easy to run into a wall or hit a sharp edge. If we're dating in the dark, we run the risk of going to places we shouldn't go.

A boundary is a visible or invisible line that marks a limit. The idea is not to go beyond the point set by the boundary. Why do we need boundaries in dating?

Setting Boundaries in Dating

Most couples get boundaries all wrong because they ask the wrong questions. Often when we think about boundaries, we think that the term refers only to not sleeping with the person we are dating. We think only about physical restraints. As a result, when we talk about boundaries, we are usually talking about sex. Too often, that's the only kind of boundary couples set. Nothing else is off limits. They don't set a limit and just let the relationship flow, but that's wrong.

My dad told me two things to remember in life, and I have never forgotten them. The first was that he would kill me if he ever heard or smelled that I had smoked mariju-ana—and I believed him because he slept with a machete under his bed. The second thing he told me had to do with dreadlocks in my hair. Back then, the idea of dreadlocks was attached to a person being a thief, a rebel, or some other type of criminal. Dad said, "If I ever catch you in dreadlocks, you are going to die."

Importantly, he never specifically told me that I couldn't smoke marijuana or wear dreadlocks. Instead of placing boundaries on *me*, he clearly communicated *his* limits as my father, as well as the consequences if I were to transgress those limits—even if those consequences were excessive. As Christian psychologists Dr. Henry Cloud and Dr. John Townsend emphasize in their series on boundaries in relationships, boundaries represent a healthy and biblical way to define ourselves and our per-sonal limits, not a means of controlling others.[5]

Unfortunately, as far as I knew, anything besides ma-rijuana and dreadlocks was okay because my father only set those two specific limits, ignoring many other areas that might have required me to place boundaries on my-self.

We need to ask broader questions to help set bounda-ries in dating. These questions include:

- What are we really after in dating?
- What's the goal? What are we trying to secure in dating?
- What do we want to enjoy in our dating relationship?
- What is our definition of success in this endeavor?

When I started dating, I had energy and a desire to experience more in life, but I determined that I wasn't going to play games. I said, "I'm never going to hurt the woman I date." Not everyone thinks that way. When I said those words, my goal was to try to keep the woman I was dating pure. It's important to set goals for our dating relationships. Our primary goal should be to honor our covenant with God above all else. One way to do this is to take a vow together before God to remain sexually pure before marriage.

When I said that I wanted to keep the woman I dated pure, I wasn't just talking about sex, but also her mind. We can corrupt someone else's mind. This happens when we play games in dating. A better approach is to work together to make godly decisions about what is and is not okay in our relationship based on God's Word.

Illusions About Boundaries

Boundaries are hard to keep because Satan tries to convince us that we are only sacrificing and not getting anything in return. Satan wants the wrong relationship for us because if he can connect us in the wrong relationship, he can ruin our purpose in life. Satan makes us think that our pure relationships are like slavery and bondage. We think that others are enjoying a freedom in their physical relationships that is denied us. We feel that we aren't free in our relationships. When those thoughts come into our minds, we need to be aware that our enemy, Satan, may be planting them.

Another illusion we may face regarding boundaries relates to the positive limits God calls us to set in our relationships. It's okay for our partner to be our best friend. It's okay to enjoy doing things together. It's important to secure the things we enjoy about our dating relationship. We secure these benefits when we follow God's leading in the relationship, without giving in to the world's opinion that such a relationship is dysfunctional.

It's easy to think that something is wrong with you if you aren't in a dating relationship. You may wonder why you can't get a catch. There may be many different reasons God has not yet placed you in a dating relationship. Being willing to turn on the light will help you to see and acknowledge what may be going on.

A person you want to date may not be ready to enter a dating relationship. We've discussed the role that having a relationship with God plays in a healthy relationship. Perhaps the other person doesn't yet have that saving relationship with Jesus Christ. Furthermore, not everyone who is saved is mature enough personally or emotionally to date in the way defined in this book.

As Christians, we believe that God has a plan and a

purpose for our lives. If He hasn't led you into a dating relationship in the timing that you would like, perhaps there is something else you're supposed to be doing. Tiffany wanted to be in a dating relationship. She wanted to feel secure and connected to another person in a meaningful way. Her previous boyfriend had broken up with her, saying that the relationship wasn't the best fit for him. Friends counseled Tiffany to focus on finding a good job and strengthening her relationships with family and others. Tiffany was wise to trust God and follow His leading, preparing herself to be someone who would be able to thrive in an emotionally healthy relationship in God's perfect timing. In the meantime, she could grow in her nonromantic relationships, gaining valuable insights and emotional maturity.

Types of Boundaries in a Dating Relationship

A healthy dating relationship requires emotional boundaries. Boundaries are often associated with the wrong emotions. We want to give too much—emotionally and physically—too quickly. We become more than friends but less than spouses so fast, not allowing time for the relationship to grow naturally. The relationship becomes stuck in that in-between status when we don't allow God to guide our emotions. Solomon, a very wise man, cautioned his sons, "Guard your heart above all else, for it determines the course of your life" (Proverbs 4:23). We have to give our emotions to God and let Him guide them.

Second, we need to set boundaries around our

expectations. We expect too much too quickly. One person may come from a background where it's not supposed to go that way. One person may expect the relationship to develop more slowly than the other person does. Two people may not have the same expectations regarding behavior in a dating relationship, levels of commitment, or even setting boundaries.

A third boundary involves talking about the future. It's okay to talk about personal goals and plans for the future when we first meet someone; that's part of getting to know another person. However, both people really need to have the same level of commitment before they can talk about the future in terms of building one together. Once both people commit themselves to a serious dating relationship and moving forward together, they can talk about their future as a couple.

The boundary we expect to set in a dating relationship is that of sexuality. In a relationship founded on God's Word, the expectation will be to follow God's standard. If there is a question on that, knowing early in the relationship prevents the couple from wasting time. Turn on the light and set this boundary with care and determination; it's too easy to fool ourselves. Once both people agree on the boundary, live as children of light. Paul described it this way: "So put to death the sinful, earthly things lurking within you. Have nothing to do with sexual immorality, impurity, lust, and evil desires" (Colossians 3:5). Turn away from these things.

> *Since God chose you to be the holy people he loves, you must clothe yourselves with tenderhearted mercy,*

kindness, humility, gentleness, and patience. Make allow-
ance for each other's faults, and forgive anyone who
offends you. Remember, the Lord forgave you, so you must
forgive others. Above all, clothe yourselves with love, which
binds us all together in perfect harmony.
—Colossians 3:12–14

Let's say a couple has sought maturity in their dating relationship. They have pursued personal growth and have begun to build a strong commitment to one another. They have chosen to set godly boundaries and have submitted their relationship to God. These actions place them in a position for healthy bonding to take place. Rather than separating the two people, healthy boundaries can bind a couple together in unity and help them to develop a strong dating relationship that prepares them for the possibility of marriage.

WORKBOOK

Chapter Eight Questions

Question: What are some ways, other than premarital sex, that people get hurt through a lack of boundaries in dating? How can the right boundaries actually help you to enjoy a relationship more fully?

_____

_____

_____

_____

_____

_____

_____

_____

_____

_____

_____

Question: Do you feel pressure to be in a relationship even if you are not personally ready or if God has not brought a qualified partner into your life? What are some ways to approach a period of unwanted singleness with purpose, intention, and dedication to Christ?

_____

_____

_____

_____

_____

_____

_____

_____

_____

_____

_____

Action: Write down a list of healthy boundaries for your dating relationships. If you are currently dating, this is a good exercise to do together to determine if you are at the same level of maturity and to compare your expectations. Remember that boundaries should apply to the physical, mental, emotional, and spiritual aspects of the relationship. Are your boundaries based on God's Word and the wisdom of mentors? Are they based on God's grace, His goodness, and the truth of His Word, or are they based on your feelings, cultural norms, or legalism?

_____

_____

_____

_____

_____

_____

_____

_____

_____

_____

_____

Chapter Eight Notes

_____

_____

_____

_____

_____

_____

_____

_____

_____

_____

_____

_____

_____

_____

_____

_____

_____

_____

_____

_____

CHAPTER NINE

Bonding

When two people first meet, before they even commit to a dating relationship, the bonding process begins. Bonding begins when two people first make a connection. We connect with someone else when we first meet the other person. Any time we meet someone new, we form a first impression of that person. We observe, try to understand something about him or her, and form an opinion, right or wrong.

If we are favorably impressed with that person, we may decide that we would like to get to know him or her better. At the same time, we may hesitate, concerned that we will be rejected. We can reassure ourselves by taking it slow, thinking about a good strategy to introduce ourselves or engage that person in conversation. We think about what clue would indicate our interest and consider the best way to deliver that hint.

One person approaches the other, and the two begin talking. At this point, they may exchange contact information. What *shouldn't* happen at this stage is making out or having sex, but this is often a modern reality. How can couples who want to follow God's purpose in their dating relationship avoid this situation? It's not too early to discuss and set clear physical boundaries in the relationship. This is the time to be honest with one another and make sure that neither person is playing games.

The couple agrees to go out on a date. Often the man asks the woman out. Tradition would caution a woman not to give herself away too easily. In reality, though, either person can trip up the other one by overstepping godly boundaries.

Bonding and Boundaries

This is why setting boundaries in relationships and understanding the bonding process go hand in hand. We cannot go completely through the one process in order without taking corresponding steps in the other process. As the couple walks through the bonding process, they will set boundaries at each step relevant to their current level of commitment. We need to revisit boundaries concerning emotions, expectations, discussions about the future, and sexuality at each stage of the bonding process. Boundary-setting is not a one-and-done or a one-size-fits-all experience. Therefore, it is important for couples exploring a dating relationship to do so in the light of God's Word.

Initially, both people need to be very careful about how much they share with the other person. A strong relationship is built on trust, which requires a level of commitment that develops through the bonding process. If one person or both people share in ways that are inappropriate for their current level of commitment, the potential for misunderstandings or emotional or spiritual damage is greater. For example, if Austin shares details about his home life with Kaitlyn before bonding has taken place, she may not keep the confidence in the same way she would if they were bonded and committed to one another at a deeper level.

Bonding takes place face to face. When we look into another person's eyes and engage with him or her in conversation, we achieve a greater level of understanding than we would through solely auditory (telephone) or digital (email, text, or message) communication. When we meet in person, we see and hear the other person; we observe gestures and facial expressions. All of this adds meaning to what that person says.

As important as meeting face to face is, you have to be careful with intimate touching. If you have set godly physical boundaries on the relationship from the beginning, that will prove helpful at this stage. In a serious dating relationship, you need to be sensitive to and follow God's leading in the matter of touching. This applies in any dating situation: at the movies, in the car, whenever you are alone together.

God's Word gives guidance in some areas and specifics in others. In the gray areas, such as kissing, couples will have to consider the consequence. Which behaviors naturally lead to things that are reserved only for married couples? When is light kissing appropriate? When may a couple move to deep kissing? At what point does light touching become serious touching that leads to sex?

Another thing to consider regarding physical boundaries in a relationship is where the relationship is in the bonding process. For bonding to happen, there first has to be a strong commitment between the two people. Friends and family members may observe a couple holding hands and assume that some chemistry has started to occur in the relationship.

Bonding and Rejection

The very nature of the bonding process brings with it the possibility of rejection. Either person may be worried about rejection, especially if one person is waiting for the other to make a move. This applies throughout the bonding process, not only when two people first meet. If a man doesn't take a woman's hand or lean in to kiss her, she may feel it as rejection. If a man says, "I love you," is he only trying to get her to bed? In that case, her rejection would be well founded!

Bonding and God's Design

The idea that sex before marriage is not a sin is the social norm of the day. This is part of the culture in which we live. This is not a Christian norm, and it is not true within the Christian culture. In fact, in the song Solomon wrote to his beloved, he wrote this refrain three times in eight short chapters: "Promise me, O women of Jerusalem, by the gazelles and wild deer, not to awaken love until the time is right" (Song of Solomon 2:7). The New

International Version adds the word "arouse" to this admonition.

In God's design for covenant relationships, there's a good reason for these cautions. Jesus said, "'God made them male and female' from the beginning of creation. 'This explains why a man leaves his father and mother and is joined to his wife, and the two are united into one.' Since they are no longer two but one, let no one split apart what God has joined together" (Mark 10:6–9). This passage refers to divorce, which takes place after a couple is married, but it also explains why sex has a place only in marriage. The more closely a couple bonds, the harder it is to separate if they determine that the relationship is a misfit, which is something that may happen *before* marriage. In other words, since there is a possibility of separating before marriage, a couple should not be joined in physical relationship before marriage.

Throughout the bonding process, it is important to evaluate your dating relationship in terms of boundaries and the level of commitment each person has to the relationship. This is also the time to consider and evaluate potential red flags and warnings that may indicate that the relationship is not on solid ground.

WORKBOOK

Chapter Nine Questions

Question: Describe a time when you allowed yourself to bond with another person too closely too soon. What motivated you to throw caution to the wind? Were you simply naive, or were you desperate for love and acceptance? Were there painful consequences for this unhealthy bonding, and if so, what were they?

_____

_____

_____

_____

_____

_____

_____

_____

_____

Question: What are some reasons a person may be unable to bond emotionally, even with someone in whom he or she is deeply interested? How can this fear of intimacy be addressed during the single season? What is the danger of entering a marriage when one partner is unable to bond correctly or is looking to the other person to heal his or her hurts?

_____

_____

_____

_____

_____

_____

_____

_____

_____

_____

_____

Action: Glue two pieces of different-colored paper together and leave them to dry overnight. In the morning, try to separate them. What is the result? How is this an object lesson of the "cleaving" that God has designed for marriage and the damage that can be done when people bond through premarital sex, only to break up later? On one of the ripped papers, write a paraphrase of Song of

Solomon 2:7 and keep it as a reminder of the importance of waiting for God's timing in the bonding process.

_____

_____

_____

_____

_____

_____

_____

_____

_____

_____

Chapter Nine Notes

_____

_____

_____

_____

_____

_____

_____

_____

_____

_____

_____

_____

_____

_____

_____

_____

_____

_____

_____

_____

_____

_____

Part Three: Evaluate

CHAPTER TEN

Red Flags in a Dating Relationship

We look at our shoes in the light to determine if they are appropriate for the task at hand. Have you equipped yourself properly to enter a dating relationship? Once you have committed to that relationship, is it a good fit for you as you go about your task of living for God as one of His children? We also look at our shoes in the light to make sure that they are appropriate for the weather. In this case, is the relationship sturdy and able to withstand the storms of life?

Turning to God's Word to shed light on a dating relationship will help you to answer these questions. You date to learn about another person. Dating is not the time to avoid the hard topics as you get to know the other person's history, weaknesses, ambitions, beliefs, and values. What you see—for example, life habits—may not change. If you choose to ignore red flags, it may be to your detriment.

A red flag is a warning signal. It indicates danger or an action that should be stopped. If you do not pay attention to red flags in a dating relationship, you are moving recklessly toward an accident. Instead of ignoring these signs, you should use them to evaluate the fit and overall health of the relationship.

Lack of Personal Spiritual Growth

For Christians, the most obvious red flag is also the most important. Is the other person committed to Jesus Christ as his or her Savior and Lord? If not, do not engage with this person; it only leads to trouble in a relationship. Do not hesitate to shed light on this area of a dating relationship to see if there is a misfit! Paul said plainly, "Don't team up with those who are unbelievers. How can righteousness be a partner with wickedness? How can light live with darkness? ... How can a believer be a partner with an unbeliever?" (2 Corinthians 6:14–15).

We cannot join together in such a close relationship with someone who is not part of Christ as we are part of Christ. The time to make sure that the other person is a believer is now, during the dating relationship, before you become so committed to each other that it is difficult to break apart.

Other red flags to watch for include lack of maturity, lack of responsibility, and lack of vision in the relationship. Let's bring these topics into the light and examine them.

Lack of Maturity in the Relationship

Lack of maturity may be demonstrated by either person. A man may be a "momma's boy." God commands us, "Honor your father and mother" (Exodus 20:12). Jesus clarified our priorities when He said that "a man leaves his father and mother and is joined to his wife, and the two are united into one" (Matthew 19:5). If a man loves his mom more than his spouse, his mom will always be placed ahead of his wife, even after marriage.

A person may be looking for someone to take care of him or her. He or she may not have experienced love at home and may never have been nurtured. This person may have wanted the love of his or her parents but never received it. A woman may want a man who will protect her, but some men take this too far and become overbearing or controlling in the relationship. A man may refuse to grow up. This type of man is a magnet for a good-spirited, nurturing woman who wants to take care of him.

Sometimes people bring insecurities to a relationship. These insecurities may include lack of confidence, excessive need for acceptance, or lack of self-worth. Sometimes (not always) a person will address these feelings by flirting with the opposite sex. This can show a lack of maturity, which, in turn, affects the dating relationship. Another behavior insecure people may engage in is excessive use of social media. This can be a way to seek approval and acceptance from others, and it can also indicate immaturity in a relationship. Excessive use of social media shows a lack of willingness to act responsibly.

Lack of Willingness to Act Responsibly

An important aspect of maturity is the willingness and ability to act responsibly. Does each person in the relationship take responsibility for his or her actions? Maturity also includes an awareness of other people. Paul instructed his readers, "Don't look out only for your own interests, but take an interest in others, too" (Philippians 2:4).

Shining a light on a relationship helps us to take a closer look. It shows us things we may not see if we choose to remain in the dark. Acting responsibly in a dating relationship encompasses a variety of behaviors. Keeping secrets from the other person indicates a lack of trust, which affects the overall health of the relationship.

Traditional views of husband and wife place the husband in the role of a protector and provider. This concept is based on Paul's instruction to husbands:

> *For husbands, this [submitting to one another] means love your wives, just as Christ loved the church. He gave up his life for her.... In the same way, husbands ought to love their wives as they love their own bodies. For a man who loves his wife actually shows love for himself. No one hates his own body but feeds and cares for it, just as Christ cares for the church.*
> *—Ephesians 5:25, 28–29*

Putting these two ideas together, we see that one qualification for a committed dating relationship is for a man to have a means of providing for himself. If the relationship leads to marriage, he will then be in a position to provide for his spouse. That is not to say that the entire financial burden will rest on him; in our current day, that may not be possible. This issue is more a matter of heart intention than a specific level of income. Does the man have the desire to treat a potential wife in the way Paul described above?

In this context, for women to act responsibly means to "submit to your husbands as to the Lord. For a husband is the head of his wife as Christ is the head of the church. He is the Savior of his body, the church. As the church submits to Christ, so you wives should submit to your husbands in everything" (Ephesians 5:22–24). The best explanation of how this works is seen in Paul's earlier words: "...submit to one another out of reverence for Christ" (Ephesians 5:21). In Christ, men and women have different roles in the relationship. Acting responsibly is a "one another" endeavor, and it takes vision and commitment.

Lack of Vision in the Relationship

Vision refers to the ability to look ahead. We shine a light to see what's ahead on the path we're walking. One of the goals in a dating relationship is to learn to listen to each other. It's a time of learning more about each other and becoming more committed to the relationship. As noted at the beginning of this chapter, this is a time to have conversations about where each person is coming from on a variety of topics. This enables us to identify potential red flags that may affect the future of the relationship.

For example, two people may have differences in

lifestyle. One person may enjoy extensive travel while the other does not. One person may be a day person while the other is a night person. One person may be an introvert while the other is an extrovert. They may interact with other people in very different ways. One person may decide that he or she cannot tolerate the way the other person does things in a certain area. It's also important to have conversations about each person's perspective on money (spending versus saving), raising kids, and roles in a relationship that leads to marriage.

Wise couples will go slowly in developing their physical connection, making sure to clarify the vision of where the relationship is going. If one person in the relationship chooses not to understand and agree with this caution, he or she isn't committed. It shows that he or she doesn't care about the relationship. That person may be saying, "My way or the highway. If you don't do it this way (get more physical than is appropriate), there's the highway." That's a red flag. Be mindful of reaction versus action. Don't give in to the pressure of the moment.

At the beginning of this book, we discussed the role of emotions in our relationships. Emotions play positive as well as negative roles. They can strengthen a relationship or do great harm, as we'll see in the next chapter.

WORKBOOK

Chapter Ten Questions

Question: Examine your walk with Christ, your maturity, your responsibility, and your vision for the future (including your future marriage). Are you truly ready to be in a committed relationship, or do you have some work to do first?

_____

_____

_____

_____

_____

_____

_____

_____

_____

Question: Read about the biblical roles of husband and wife in Ephesians 5. Are you prepared to take on the responsibilities that God has given to a Christian husband or wife? If you are currently in a relationship, do you and your partner have the same understanding of and commitment to these biblical roles that God has set forth for you?

_____

_____

_____

_____

_____

_____

_____

_____

_____

_____

_____

_____

Action: Look at a picture of a yoke. Imagine two different kinds of animals in the yoke together, each trying to go its own way. While we typically use the phrase "unequally yoked" to refer to a believer marrying a non-believer, what are some other areas where it is important to be as alike as possible in your vision for life?

_____

_____

_____

_____

_____

_____

_____

_____

_____

_____

_____

_____

Chapter Ten Notes

CHAPTER ELEVEN

The Power of Emotions

Emotions can themselves be red flags in a dating relationship. Moreover, it's important to know how a potential partner deals with strong and negative emotions.

Anger

Anger is a strong emotion of irritation. It arises when a need or expectation is not met. It can range from mild irritation to an uncontrolled explosion of rage. It can also involve a desire for revenge. There may be a sense of fury that destroys all common sense. When people get to this point, there is a very real danger that they will destroy anyone or anything in the path of their anger. The inability or unwillingness to manage our anger is an extremely important red flag!

Solomon advised, "Make no friendship with an angry man; and with a furious man thou shalt not go" (Proverbs 22:24 KJV). This is wise advice, as anger is a challenging emotion, especially when it comes to close relationships. Anger management issues can apply to women as well as men. In either case, be mindful of actions versus reactions. For example, observe how a potential date reacts to anger. Does the person act or react? Potential partners need to be able to handle their anger properly. Be careful not to add hot air to an "anger balloon." A person with unresolved anger issues can blow up the relationship. People become fearful when there is a situation fueled by anger because the "anger balloon" could explode.

Anger comes from various sources. It may come from a wounded heart or a feeling of injustice. People get angry when church leaders lead double lifestyles. Others get angry when they feel disrespected.

Fear and anger often go hand in hand. When someone is afraid of the outcome of a situation, he or she may express anger to mask the fear. Or, as noted above, when there is anger in a situation, one person may become afraid—sometimes rightfully so.

Some anger comes from a desire to condemn or get revenge. This type of anger is sinful. People may be stubborn in their anger, refusing to alter their stance or consider a different perspective. Sometimes anger stays with a person a long time in the form of a grudge.

Abuse

Sometimes negative emotions lead to damaging behavior, such as abuse. It would be wise to turn on the light to check for signs of potential abuse at the beginning of the relationship. Does the person use unnecessary strength when giving hugs or cuddles?

Even if a relationship hasn't progressed very far physically, there may still be signs of potential abuse. Does the other person show a tendency toward jealousy or possessive behavior? These attitudes can lead to emotional or verbal abuse. Other attitudes to watch for include blaming, resentment, sarcasm, deceit, or a sense of superiority or entitlement.

The earlier in a dating relationship you can identify a misfit, the easier it will be to depart from the relationship, as I discussed in chapter 4. Red flags function as beacons in the dark to help us spot potential problem areas. If, in spite of the warning signals, you want to continue to put effort into the relationship, you can bring the matter before God in prayer.

The need for prayer and wise counsel is why the church is so important in our lives. So many people are getting it wrong. We are the light of the world, and we need to take the gospel of Jesus Christ into the world.

WORKBOOK

Chapter Eleven Questions

Question: Do you know how to manage your anger in a healthy way? When you are upset, do you tend to take it out on those around you? How does your partner respond to stress, frustration, and difficulties? What do those who have known your partner for a long time say about his or her temper?

_____

_____

_____

_____

_____

_____

_____

_____

_____

Question: What fears and anxieties do you struggle with? How might these negatively affect a dating relationship? How can you take your insecurities to God and allow His healing and peace into your life?

_____

_____

_____

_____

_____

_____

_____

_____

_____

_____

_____

Action: Look around your church and identify:

- Marriages that are honoring to God and that you want to emulate
- Mentors who have wisdom to offer you in your current season

- Friends who can hold you accountable and encourage you in keeping your commitments throughout the dating season and as you evaluate a potential spouse.

How will you allow each of these a place in your life to speak truth, offer hope, and uphold you in prayer?

_____

_____

_____

_____

_____

_____

_____

_____

_____

_____

_____

Chapter Eleven Notes

Frequently Asked Questions About Christian Dating

I've been in ministry a long time. As I mentioned in the introduction, I've served in youth ministry for nineteen years. During that time, I've also provided pre-marital and marital counseling. You can imagine that I get asked a lot of questions. I've done my best to address the most common dating issues for Christians in this book, but there are many other questions that are relevant for Christians who do not want to date in the dark. The following are some of the most common.

1. *Should I ever date someone who is not a Christian?* In chapter 10, we noted that a lack of personal spiritual growth is a red flag in a dating relationship. Consider how long a relationship will last that is constructed on a foundation of different values. Our values affect the way we live, which becomes part of our culture. Abraham sent his servant to find a wife for Isaac from Abraham's people, not a foreigner. A generation later, Isaac commanded his

son Jacob, "You must not marry any of these Canaanite women" (Genesis 28:1). In terms of spirituality, we should not enter into a relationship with someone who is from a different spiritual culture or a different faith. Anyone we date should be a believer in Jesus Christ.

2. *Should I marry someone who is not a Christian and then trust God to save him or her?* No, definitely not. Paul had different advice for someone who married as an unbeliever and then became a believer, while his or her spouse did not (1 Corinthians 7:12–16).

3. *Should I live with the person I am dating so I can get to know him or her better?* Absolutely not. We should not create a marital situation before we are ready and before the relationship has reached that point. We already have a good name for this situation: marriage. Don't live with someone before marriage.

4. *Is it okay to flirt with married people?* No, never. Jesus made it very clear. He said, "You have heard the commandment that says, 'You must not commit adultery.' But I say, anyone who even looks at a woman with lust has already committed adultery with her in his heart" (Matthew 5:27–28). Married people should show the ring on their finger to any flirtatious person.

5. *Should I date a person who is separated?* The person is still married! Until the divorce is final, dating such a person creates an adulterous affair.

6. *Is it okay for a woman to initiate a relationship with a man?* No, it is not. Possibly the best foundation for this principle is seen in Paul's words to wives and husbands: "For a husband is the head of his wife as Christ is the head of the church" (Ephesians 5:23). Men have a certain

amount of God-given authority over women, though it should be exercised in a Christlike way. Therefore, a woman can give hints and clues to a man, but she should not ask directly for a relationship with a man. Instead, drop him a hint! Women are hinters; men are hunters.

7. *Will God send me a spouse who is unattractive?* Sometimes we see a guy with a girl and wonder, "How can she be with a man who looks like that?" However, they are perfect for each other. They are attracted to each other. God will give you the person who is perfect for you. You will have a unique connection with that person. I still love my wife after twenty-two years because God sent her to me. God knows what attracts us, and He will bring each of us the right person.

8. *Is it okay to date online?* We live in a new age of technology. If two people take the time to get to know one another, meeting someone online is fine. If a man or a woman finds the right person and marries him or her, God's blessing can still be on the relationship.

9. *Should I date a person who is ten years older than I am? What is an appropriate age difference between two people?* An age difference between two people need not be a hindrance. Some people need someone who is older. The one who is older helps the younger person to mature a bit. The younger person offers life, energy, and vitality to the relationship. They can balance each other's needs.

10. *At what age should a child be allowed to start dating?* Don't set a specific age. Consider instead the person's maturity level, along with other factors discussed in this book.

11. *Is it okay to talk with my kids about sex?* Of course

it is okay to discuss sex with your children. We need to educate and equip our children with knowledge. Don't be ashamed or embarrassed. Kids today learn about dating and relationships from the media, the internet, and many other sources. The Bible, our standard, instructs us, "Don't copy the behavior and customs of this world, but let God transform you into a new person by changing the way you think. Then you will learn to know God's will for you, which is good and pleasing and perfect" (Romans 12:2).

Chapter Twelve Notes

_____

_____

_____

_____

_____

_____

_____

_____

_____

_____

_____

_____

_____

_____

_____

_____

_____

_____

_____

_____

_____

_____

_____

_____

CONCLUSION

Honor God

When you enter a dating relationship, it's good to remember that God is a covenant-keeping God. He also wants us to keep our covenants with one another, especially after marriage. The best way to do this is to educate yourself about the dating relationship, equip yourself to approach this relationship with God's purpose in mind, and evaluate the health and overall fit of the relationship. It's important to remember that God's design for dating is to find the best person for you to make a lifelong commitment to in marriage.

In this book, we've looked at several ways to evaluate a dating relationship objectively. Feelings play an important role in how we interact with other people. Emotions and stress impact our relationships in different ways. Prayer can have a positive impact by strengthening a dating relationship. Before dating someone, you first need to connect in relationship with God. This will enable you to form healthy spiritual, physical, and soulful connections in a dating relationship when the time and circumstances are right.

A lack of maturity can affect the health of a dating relationship. You would do well to consider your own, as well as a potential partner's, maturity because dating is designed to be preparation for marriage. If you intend to enter a dating relationship with this purpose in mind, there are specific things you can do to equip yourself. You can observe and evaluate the other person using several tests. You should apply these same tests to yourself to determine if there are any action steps you need to take to become a godly partner for another person. Understanding potential pitfalls is another way you can equip yourself to enter a dating relationship. Sometimes working with a mentor can be beneficial in this process.

Once you decide to enter a dating relationship, you will want to set healthy boundaries. At the same time, you are entering a bonding process with another person. Bonding is a critical component of building a healthy dating relationship that leads to marriage. At each step along the way, you and your partner should evaluate where you are in the bonding process and set new or different boundaries.

You should look closely at the relationship to evaluate it and determine if there are any red flags, or warning signs. Improper perspectives, attitudes, and actions in many of the areas already discussed can be red flags in the relationship. Emotions are powerful and can also be red flags.

Often questions arise in the process of equipping ourselves and evaluating our relationships. In the last chapter, I addressed some of the most common questions I've heard in my work with couples, but you may have others. This is why it's important to find godly mentors, to stay connected to your church, and to seek God's will through prayer and Scripture study.

Throughout this book, we've compared the process of dating to turning on the light so we can better see what shoes we should wear for the right fit and purpose. We need to see clearly to determine how well two people fit each other in a relationship. Ryan and Elizabeth dated and then married because their first impression was that they felt comfortable with each other, like a pair of old shoes. He's the right shoe, and she's the left shoe. They just go together. Turn on the light to make sure that the person you want to date is a good fit. When shoes fit correctly, they support us as we walk through life.

When looking for a spouse, Christians should seek to honor God in the dating process. We do things His way, as specified in the Bible, because we want our relationships to glorify Him. Marriage, the Word of God tells us, is a metaphor for Christ and the Church. The end goal of Christian dating is a godly marriage that points others to Christ as husband and wife love each other sacrificially and serve God together, living as one for Him.

About the Author

Pastor Kenneth Harper was born and raised on the beautiful Island of Trinidad and has distinguished himself as a man who has a personal relationship with Jesus Christ. He is devoted to a lifelong commitment and partnership with his lovely wife, Lady Gail Harper, and the love and adoration of their three children: Kandice, Keegan and Kylia.

Pastor Harper gave his life to Christ on June 20, 1987, at the Trinidad Christian Center under the Apostleship of Dr. Austin J. De Bourg. Shortly after his salvation experience,

Pastor Harper came to the United States, later settling in Baltimore, MD. God placed a call to preach the Gospel of Jesus Christ on his life, but he initially resisted. In 1987, he began attending Christian Life Church, where he met his wife, Gail Harper. They were married on November 18, 1989.

God's call to preach was confirmed again in 1989. A few short years later, Pastor Harper attended Arlington Bible College and served under the leadership of Pastor J. Luther Carroll at Christian Life Church, where he was ordained a full-time Minister of the Gospel in 1994.

In fulfillment of the Great Commission, Pastor Harper has preached the Good News around the world and regularly supports missions in various countries throughout the world, including Laos, Guatemala, and South Africa.

In the year 2000, he was ordained a Minister of the Church of God (Cleveland, Tennessee), and in 2003, he received his calling from God to establish a church. That same year, Pastor Harper established himself in the community as a minority business owner and successful entrepreneur, and he continues to provide jobs to many whom others consider unemployable because of past mistakes and indiscretions.

In 2006, God increased Pastor Harper's desire to respond to His call. By faith, in August of 2009, Pastor Harper moved forward in establishing Channel of Grace Worship Center Inc., where he currently serves as President and Lead Pastor. Today, among other responsibilities, he continues to minister to marriages and to mentor youth and young adults while cultivating various philanthropic endeavors throughout his local and global communities.

REFERENCES

Notes

1. "Psychology Topics: Marriage and Divorce." American Psychological Association. https://www.apa.org/topics/divorce/.

2. Zodiates, Spiros. *The Complete Word Study Dictionary: New Testament*. AMG Publishers, 1992, p. 1495.

3. Schumacher, Helene. "Why More Men Than Women Die by Suicide." BBC. March 17, 2019. https://www.bbc.com/future/article/20190313-why-more-men-kill-themselves-than-women.

4. Swaminathan, Nikhil. "Gender Jabber: Do Women Talk More Than Men?" Scientific American. July 6, 2007. https://www.scientificamerican.com/article/women-talk-more-than-men/.

5. Cloud, Henry, and John Townsend. *Boundaries in Dating: Making Dating Work*. Zondervan, 2001.

Made in the USA
Middletown, DE
21 March 2021